CHILD DEVELOPMENT THROUGH THE EYES OF CHILDREN'S AUTHORS

USING PICTURE BOOKS TO UNDERSTAND THEORY

Cory Cooper Hansen

Arizona State University

Debby Zambo

Arizona State University

PEARSON

Merrill
Prentice Hall

Upper Saddle River, New Jersey
Columbus, Ohio

Vice President and Executive Publisher: Jeffery W. Johnston
Publisher: Kevin M. Davis
Development Editor: Autumn Crisp Benson
Editorial Assistant: Sarah N. Kenoyer
Production Editor: Mary Harlan
Design Coordinator: Diane C. Lorenzo
Cover Design: Bryan Huber
Production Manager: Laura Messerly
Director of Marketing: David Gesell
Marketing Manager: Autumn Purdy
Marketing Coordinator: Brian Mounts

This book was set in Comic Sans by Pearson Education. It was printed and bound by Bind Rite Graphics. The cover was printed by The Lehigh Press, Inc.

Pearson Prentice Hall™ is a trademark of Pearson Education, Inc.
Pearson® is a registered trademark of Pearson plc
Prentice Hall® is a registered trademark of Pearson Education, Inc.
Merrill® is a registered trademark of Pearson Education, Inc.

Pearson Education Ltd.   Pearson Education Australia Pty. Limited
Pearson Education Singapore Pte. Ltd.   Pearson Education North Asia Ltd.
Pearson Education Canada, Ltd.   Pearson Educación de Mexico, S.A. de C.V.
Pearson Education–Japan   Pearson Education Malaysia Pte. Ltd.

10 9 8 7 6 5 4 3 2 1
ISBN: 0-13-199363-1

PREFACE

This book is intended as a companion text to Teresa M. McDevitt and Jeanne Ellis Ormrod's *Child Development and Education*, Third Edition, © 2007. As part of the Merrill Education Student Enrichment Series, this supplement was written specifically to serve as a resource for instructors who have adopted the McDevitt and Ormrod text for use in courses that deal with child development, educational psychology, or a similar discipline. More specifically, it was written to help students in teacher preparation and other professional programs make connections between what they learn in their child development classes and what these theories and principles look like in real-life situations through the medium of children's literature.

Each chapter identifies two picture books with specific connections to theory and principles, along with questions to encourage open discussion, critical thinking, and problem solving. The picture books suggested were carefully selected to accurately portray child development and engage the learner, through narrative and pictures, in creating deeper understanding of developmental theories and principles. In addition, hands-on, collaborative activities promote active learning and invite students to practice their new knowledge and skills.

CONTENTS

Rationale for Supplementing the Course Text with Picture Books

Imagine this scene taking place in a child- and adolescent-development course. A college instructor is in front of 38 students, reading a children's picture book. The book is *David Gets in Trouble* by David Shannon (2002). All the students' eyes and ears are on her and the whole room is laughing and engaged. After examining each illustration and reading each page, the instructor poses questions to spark discussion about David, the main character who always manages an excuse for his behavior. The students' replies indicate that they are connecting the story to what they have read in their college textbook and to their experiences with children. For example, after reading the page where David tells his teacher that the dog ate his homework, one student comments that the daily checklist for homework completion in the textbook might be a good strategy for David to use. Another suggests that David could check off steps he had completed and learn to administer self-reinforcement. Someone else thinks David just needs a good spanking.

Opening our college courses with a "read-aloud" and using picture books in our courses has become a pleasant and expected ritual by our students. When we use picture books, our students see theory in practice as they interpret characters' actions, analyze illustrations for clues, and relate the behaviors of storybook characters to the children they know. This guide introduces our favorite picture books and activities; ones that are sure to encourage discussion, challenge thinking, and promote active involvement. The authors of this guide appreciate McDevitt and Ormrod's practical suggestions for working with children. This guide joins their vision to make learning meaningful, enjoyable, and motivating for individuals who plan future careers with children and adolescents.

Chapter 1:
Making a Difference in the Lives of Children and Adolescents

Related Picture Book: *The Wild Boy* by Mordicai Gerstein

"He lived completely alone, without mother, father, or friends.
He didn't know what a mother or father was…
He didn't know what people were. He was completely wild."

Gerstein, 2002

Synopsis: Hunters (around 1800) discover a young boy who has been living wild in the mountain forests of southern France. His life becomes the focus of many scientists who pronounce him hopelessly retarded. One specialist, Dr. Itard, takes the time to help. He gives the boy a name (Victor), provides him with learning stimulation, and gives him love. With these positive factors, Victor begins to thrive; but, inside, there remains a wild boy.

Theory or Principle: Developmental theorists grapple with three overarching questions. They wonder: 1) about the influence of heredity and the environment (nature and nurture), 2) if individuals follow the same or varied paths (universality or diversity), and 3) if developmental changes are characterized by transformations or trends (qualitative and quantitative).

Materials: One copy per student of the following "nature and nuture" handout, "What would it be like for a child to grow up without any human contact?"

Directions: Begin reading *The Wild Boy.* Stop on page 19 and distribute the handout. Read the questions at the top of the page and ask students to choose the behaviors they think a child like Victor would display. When students have made their choices, discuss the changes as a group. Ask students to provide a rationale as to why they chose or rejected certain attributes. Finish reading the story.

NOTE: In fact, Victor displayed the attributes listed in the <u>right</u> column, but none on the left.

Chapter 1:
Making a Difference in the Lives of Children and Adolescents

Nature and Nurture

What would it be like for a child to grow up without any human contact?
Suppose a child like Victor grew up from birth to age twelve in a forest without any human contact. What do you think the child would be like at the age of twelve? What was Victor like when he came to live with Dr. Itard?

Place one check mark for each pair of attributes.

_____ physically weak & unhealthy   _____ physically strong & healthy

_____ attentive to stimuli   _____ inattentive to stimuli

_____ responsive to pain   _____ unresponsive to pain

_____ responsive to temperature   _____ unresponsive to temperature

_____ interested in other people   _____ uninterested in other people

_____ used gesturing language   _____ did not use gesturing language

_____ used written language   _____ did not use written language

_____ could identify colors   _____ could not identify colors

_____ had invented useful tools   _____ hadn't invented useful tools

_____ was well-mannered with people   _____ was not well-mannered with people

_____ came to feel human affection   _____ was not interested in human affection

_____ capable of eating with utensils   _____ was not capable of eating with utensils

Discussion Questions:

After the story has been read, select from the following prompts:

The relative effects of heredity and environment vary for different domains of development. What did this mean for Victor? How was this idea shown in the story?

Environment plays a greater role when conditions are extreme. How was this idea shown in the story?

Children affect their environment. Did Victor affect his environment? If so, then how?

Have students investigate average developmental features of early adolescents (10-14 years) and compare these averages to Victor's growth.

When Dr. Itard met Victor, he saw a boy who had never been held, sung to, or played with. The National Middle School Association (NMSA) recommends that every child be supported by one caring adult. Explain how the relationship between Victor and Dr. Itard met this goal. What physical, cognitive, social, and emotional changes in Victor were derived from Dr. Itard's relationship with Victor? What can we, as professionals, learn from Dr. Itard and Victor?

How is resiliency shown in the story?

Wrap up this session by having students revisit the handout and discuss it from the perspective of their new knowledge.

Chapter 1:
Making a Difference in the Lives of Children and Adolescents

Related Picture Book: *Leo the Late Bloomer* by Robert Kraus

> *"And every night Leo's father watched him for signs of blooming.
> 'Are you sure Leo's a bloomer?' asked Leo's father. 'Patience,'
> said Leo's mother. 'A watched bloomer doesn't bloom.'"*
>
> Kraus, 1971

Synopsis: Leo can't do anything right, much to the consternation of his father. Leo's mother constantly reassures her husband that Leo will catch up with the others when he is ready to eat neatly, draw, and read. Leo's father eventually gives up on him. But then, one day, in Leo's own good time, he blooms and happily announces to all that he has made it!

Theory or Principle: It is not always easy for adults to understand children's behaviors and ideas. Children who appear immature may act out or struggle and that behavior may provoke adults to focus on childrens' limitations instead of on their strengths. Accordingly, professionals who work with children need to acquire a "developmental mind-set."

Discussion Questions:
From a developmental standpoint, immaturity serves a purpose. How does this idea relate to Leo as a late bloomer?

From a developmental standpoint, the environment makes a difference. How does the factor of environment relate to Leo?

From a developmental standpoint, children face different issues today than their parents did when growing up. If Leo's father had this insight, how might it change his view of Leo?

How might focusing on Leo's strengths have helped his parents cope with his behavior? Should Leo's parents nudge him toward more advanced levels of thinking and behaving? If so, how? If not, why do you hold this point of view?

Chapter 1:
Making a Difference in the Lives of Children and Adolescents

Collaborative Learning Activity: Name Droppers

Theory or Principle: Theories are organized principles and explanations that guide the best practices for education and provide unique insights into our world. It is important that individuals who work with children and adolescents learn about various theories because, even though no one theory holds all the answers, they do provide invaluable insight into development. As a result, many courses on child development offer an introduction and broad overview of the most influential theories. The objective of this activity is to introduce students to various theories and the theorists who developed them.

Materials: For this activity, each group will need a copy of the following page (a chart), a colored piece of paper, scissors, and a glue stick.

Directions: Students work in groups of 2 - 4. Students cut out the **THEORIES** (bold, all caps, first 7 cells in the left column) and place them across the side of the colored sheet of paper. Students sort the remaining ideas and names under the proper theory.

Activity Sample:

BIOLOGICAL THEORIES	PSYCHODYNAMIC THEORIES	SOCIOCULTURAL THEORIES
Theories that focus on how genetics and physiology contribute to development.	These theories focus on the interaction between inborn traits and the environment.	
	Sigmund Freud (1924) - earliest theorist focused on internal conflicts between sexual and aggressive behaviors.	

Follow-up: After discussing where each idea or name falls, students can glue their answers down and use the chart as a study guide.

BIOLOGICAL THEORIES	Theories that focus on how genetics and physiology contribute to development.	These theories focus on the interaction between inborn traits and the environment.
BEHAVIORISM AND SOCIAL LEARNING THEORIES	Focuses on visible, external behaviors, not thought processes.	Theories that focus on how multiple factors combine to influence development.
PSYCHODYNAMIC THEORIES	Sigmund Freud (1924) – earliest theorist to focus on internal conflicts between sexual and aggressive behaviors.	Theories that pay close attention to the social and cultural context within which children live.
COGNITIVE-DEVELOPMENTAL THEORIES	Examined how children interpret and remember, and how these processes change over time.	Albert Bandura (1963) – who thought that children learn a great deal by observing others.
COGNITIVE PROCESS THEORIES	Proposed that the process of development varies from culture to culture.	Lawrence Kohlberg (1983) – stage theorist - theory of moral development.
SOCIOCULTURAL THEORIES	Jean Piaget – stage theorist who investigated children's logical thinking.	Eric Erikson (1959) – stage theorist - growth comes from internal resolution of struggles.
DEVELOPMENTAL SYSTEMS THEORIES	B. F. Skinner (1938) - children actively work for rewards and to avoid punishment.	These theories provide concrete, research-tested instructional strategies.
Focus on major transformations in the cognitive structures that underlie thinking.	Proposed that specific cultural groups encourage children to use distinct modes of thinking.	Children learn by being engaged in authentic tasks.
Urie Bronfenbrenner (1994) – systems theorist – bioecological model.	These theories propose that developmental change is influenced by the environment (nurture).	These theories capture it all – nature, nurture, and child activity.
Theories that emphasize thinking processes and how they change qualitatively over time.	Vygotsky (1934)– believed children's minds are shaped by everyday experiences in social settings.	Two key principles are that maturational levels impose limits; and that physiological states protect survival and preparing for adult roles.

BIOLOGICAL THEORIES
Theories that focus on how genetics and physiology contribute to development.
Two key principles are that maturational levels impose limits; and that physiological states protect survival and preparing for adult roles.

PSYCHODYNAMIC THEORIES
These theories focus on the interaction between inborn traits and the environment.
Sigmund Freud (1924) – earliest theorist to focus on internal conflicts between sexual and aggressive behaviors.
Eric Erikson (1959) – stage theorist - growth comes from internal resolution of struggles.

BEHAVIORISM AND SOCIAL LEARNING THEORIES
Focuses on visible, external behaviors, not thought processes.
Albert Bandura (1963) – who thought that children learn a great deal by observing others.
B. F. Skinner (1938) - children actively work for rewards and to avoid punishment. These theories propose that developmental change is influenced by the environment (nurture).

COGNITIVE-DEVELOPMENTAL THEORIES
Focus on major transformations in the cognitive structures that underlie thinking.
Lawrence Kohlberg (1983) – stage theorist - theory of moral development.
Jean Piaget – stage theorist who investigated children's logical thinking.

COGNITIVE PROCESS THEORIES
Examined how children interpret and remember, and how these processes change over time. These theories provide concrete, research-tested instructional strategies.
Theories that emphasize thinking processes and how they change qualitatively over time.

SOCIOCULTURAL THEORIES
Theories that pay close attention to the social and cultural context within which children live. Propose that the process of development varies from culture to culture.
Propose that specific cultural groups encourage children to use distinct modes of thinking.
Children learn by being engaged in authentic tasks.
Vygotsky– believed children's minds are shaped by everyday experiences in social settings.

DEVELOPMENTAL SYSTEMS THEORIES
Theories that focus on how multiple factors combine to influence development.
These theories capture it all – nature, nurture, and child activity.
Urie Bronfenbrenner (1994) – systems theorist – bioecological model.

Chapter 2: Using Research to Understand Children and Adolescents

Related Picture Book: *Alexander and the Terrible, Horrible, No Good, Very Bad Day* by Judith Viorst

> *"It has been a terrible, horrible, no good, very bad day.*
> *My mom says some days are like that."*
>
> Viorst, 1972

Synopsis: Alexander is having a terrible, horrible, no good, very bad day at home and in school. His words and the black-and-white illustrations reveal just how upset he feels.

Theory or Principle: Adults who work with children need to be astute and attuned to childrens' interests, values, and abilities. One way to gain insight into the world of children is through observation.

Materials: Copies of the following page (an observation form), one per student, and copies of the book (enough for small groups).

Directions: *Alexander and the Terrible, Horrible, No Good, Very Bad Day* contains black-and-white illustrations and words that illustrate just how upset and angry Alexander feels. Adults who work with children need to be good "kid watchers" and this book can help develop this skill. In some ways, choosing a picture-book character to observe may seem abstract and removed from watching real-life children, but there is an advantage to this technique. A snapshot of actions exists on the page so students can take their time to discover the many nuances of behavior, interactions, and emotions presented. Capturing action in the form of a picture helps students become aware of the importance of looking carefully at the children and adolescents in their lives.

Pass copies of the book out to groups of 3 – 4. Have students read it and carefully examine the illustrations. When students are finished, use the textbook to complete the observation guide.

Chapter 2: Using Research to Understand Children and Adolescents
Observation Protocol form for
Alexander and the Terrible, Horrible, No Good, Very Bad Day (Viorst, 1972)

Imagine you are going to conduct a day-long observation of Alexander. Carefully look at the pictures in the story, consider the words spoken, and use them in your observation of this terrible, horrible, no good, very bad day.

Observation	Inference

As a wrap-up, have students explain their observations and inferences. Discuss the hindrances of observing children and adolescents in real-life situations and ways to overcome those roadblocks.

Chapter 2: Using Research to Understand Children and Adolescents

Related picture book: *First Year Letters* by Julie Danneberg

> *"I'm lucky to have had such great students.*
> *I couldn't have asked for better teachers!"*

Danneberg, 2003

Synopsis: Mrs. Sarah Jane Hartwell has an interesting - and challenging - class. From loose snakes, to wild field trips, to unexpected surprises, Mrs. Hartwell faces a class full of spunky kids. In the end, her humor and hard work pay off and she learns that the reality of teaching is that *everyone* is a student and a teacher.

Theory or Principle: Action research is conducted by teachers to understand and address the challenges encountered in everyday classroom settings. Action research takes many forms (e.g., case study, whole class, program effectiveness) and follows a cycle that includes identifying a focus, collecting data, analyzing and interpreting data, and creating an action plan.

Discussion Questions: Divide students into groups of 4–5 and pose these questions: As a teacher, Mrs. Hartwell faced many challenges, just like most teachers in our classrooms today. Imagine you are a teacher like Mrs. Hartwell and design the beginning steps for an action research project. Your project can focus on a problem, a program or strategy, a school-wide issue, or an individual child. Be sure that your project contains these steps:

- Clearly state your focus in a question. Make sure what you are investigating is observable, measurable, student centered, and aimed at achievement.
- Make a connection among your focus, theories contained in this text, and research. Have others investigated a similar problem? If so, who? How? What did they find? What theory or theories contained in this text does your focus connect to, and why?
- Explain how you would collect data to gain insight into your focus question.
- Explain the ethical guidelines you would follow if you were to collect and analyze data.

Chapter 2: Using Research to Understand Children and Adolescents

Collaborative Learning Activity: Research-O

Theory or Principle: Developmental research relies on the scientific method as a means to investigate issues of interest or concern. Research is a dependable way for educators to learn about child and adolescent development. Individuals who plan careers in this field benefit from understanding various research techniques and terminology.

The objective of this activity is to introduce students to various research terms and methods.

Materials: Twenty-one 2-colored counters (or any other small markers in two colors), a copy of the Research-O playing board and playing cards (see the following pages), and scissors for each pair of students.

Directions: Students work in pairs. Have each pair:

1. Cut the Research-O playing cards apart (DO NOT CUT THE PLAYING BOARD).

2. Get twenty-one 2-colored counters.

3. Play Research-O by shuffling the playing cards and placing them in a stack. Player One turns over the first playing card (these contain definitions of terms on the board). If Player One can identify the term on the board that matches the playing card, then Player One captures the square. Take turns. The player with the most squares wins!

Collaborative Learning Activity: Research-O Playing Board (Do not cut)

ethical considerations	self-report	action research
quantitative research	test	validity
longitudinal study	scientific method	control group
qualitative research	**Research-O**	observation
experimental study	naturalistic study	reliability
interview	habituation	correlation coefficient
sample	questionnaire	cross-sectional study

Collaborative Learning Activity: Research-O Playing Cards (CUT APART)

group that does not get the treatment	extent to which data are consistent and dependable	multi-step process of answering a research question using critical thinking and analysis of evidence
research study in which data collected are predominately numerical	data collected are non-numerical	a statistic that indicates the nature of the relationship between two variables
research study in which individuals are observed in their natural environment	extent to which data-collection method assesses what it is intended to assess	the participants in a study – their performance is assumed to indicate how a larger population would perform
a treatment is introduced, other aspects of the environment are controlled, & the effect of the treatment is assessed	**Research-O**	data-collection technique whereby participants are asked to describe their own characteristics and performance
data-collection technique that uses face-to-face conversation	changes in children's physiological responses to repeated displays of the same stimulus	research study in which the performance of a single group is tracked over a period of time
data-collection technique where a researcher carefully observes and documents behavior	research study in which the performance of individuals at different ages is compared	data-collection technique that gets self-reported data through paper and pencil inventory
instrument designed to measure knowledge, understanding, and ability in a consistent fashion across individuals	systematic study of a problem/issue in one's own situation; its goal is to improve practice	informed consent, keeping work visible, accuracy, no deception, confidentiality

ethical considerations informed consent, keeping work visible, accuracy, no deception, confidentiality	**self-report** data collection technique whereby participants are asked to describe their own characteristics and performance	**action research** systematic study of a problem/issue in one's own situation, its goal is to improve practice
quantitative research a research study in which data collected are predominately numerical	**test** instrument designed to measure knowledge, understanding, and ability in a consistent fashion across individuals	**validity** extent to which data collection method assesses what it is intended to assess
longitudinal study research study in which the performance of a single group is tracked over a period of time	**scientific method** multi-step process of answering a research question using critical thinking and analysis of evidence	**control group** group that does not get the treatment
qualitative research data collected are non-numerical	**Research - O**	**observation** data collection technique where a researcher carefully observes and documents behavior
experimental study treatment is introduced, other aspects of the environment are controlled, & the effect of treatment is assessed	**naturalistic study** research study in which individuals are observed in their natural environment	**reliability** extent to which data are consistent and dependable
interview data collection technique that uses face-to-face conversation	**habituation** changes in children's physiological responses to repeated displays of the same stimulus	**correlation coefficient** a statistic that indicates the nature of the relationship between two variables
sample the participants in a study – their performance is assumed to indicate how a larger population would perform	**questionnaire** data collection technique that gets self-reported data through paper and pencil inventory	**cross-sectional study** research study in which the performance of individuals at different ages is compared

Chapter 3: Biological Beginnings

Related Picture Book: *On the Day You Were Born* by Debra Frasier

"While you waited in darkness, tiny knees curled to chin, the Earth and her creatures with the Sun and the Moon all moved in their places, each ready to greet you the very first moment of the very first day you arrived."

Frasier, 1991

Synopsis: The birth of a child not only impacts the child's immediate family, but it also affects the entire world because every person has a place on the Earth. This book is written from the perspective of the Earth as it welcomes a new member and promises to care for its people by providing trees for oxygen, gravity to hold one close, clouds for water, and day and night to structure life.

Theory or Principle: From a biological standpoint, the child is a complex, coordinated "system" with interacting parts and processes. Environmental factors influence genetic expression. Specific environmental factors that blend with heredity include nutrition, illness, medication, stressful events, temperature, exposure to light, intensity of stimulation, and opportunities for physical development. A child's specific genetic makeup is affected by at least three particular environments: passive gene-environment, evocative gene-environment, or an active gene-environment relation.

Discussion Questions: Parents-to-be often focus on the immediate environment into which they will welcome their baby. They make food and lifestyle changes, are interested in different topics, and prepare a nursery for the new member of their family. Do you think parents-to-be consider wider environmental issues? For example, do they examine the neighborhood in which their child will be raised, think ahead to preschools, or evaluate the quality of life in the city in which they live? Are these environmental issues a priority when expecting? What choices do parents have if they feel trapped in an environment that may be detrimental to the safety or well-being of their child?

The author of the story writes about the Earth as an environment for each new child and ends with an explanation of how its environment has developed people of different colors. Discuss whether adaptation for survival will continue to influence factors in heredity and environment.

Chapter 3: Biological Beginnings

Related Picture Book: *Happy Birth Day* by Robie H. Harris

"Being born must have been very hard work—seeing light, hearing new sounds, feeling air on your skin, and just being brand-new in the world. No wonder you were tired."   Harris, 1996

Synopsis: A mother tells the story of her baby's birth and shares her feelings as her baby, a whole new person, is finally placed in her arms. The story narrates what happens from different perspectives when a child enters the world: explanation of physical connections, the parents' emotional reactions to seeing, hearing, and holding their child for the first time, the role of helpers in the delivery, and how the extended family welcomes its newest member. The illustrations are exceptional!

Theory or Principle: The events leading up to and culminating in childbirth provoke a range of feelings and many changes in parents' lives. These events are managed best when families are prepared, when prenatal care has been sought, and when reasonable and realistic expectations are held about the baby's abilities and needs. As soon as babies are born, they are alert, ready for appropriate types of stimulation, and ready to be loved. To give an infant a healthy start, parents and extended family must recognize infants' abilities, interests, and styles of expression through observation and response to individual needs.

Discussion Questions:
The parents in the story seem prepared for their child. What things might they have done to be physically, cognitively, and emotionally ready for the birth experience?

This book portrays a loving family showing sensitivity to their child's needs. Find instances in the story or illustrations that illustrate these ideas:
- adults observing the sensory ability of their newborn
- adults observing the physiological state of their newborn
- parents articulating their awareness of how to soothe their child

Examine the illustrations in the book to determine the various states of arousal of the baby. What type of reflexes did the baby in the story display?

Chapter 3: Biological Beginnings

Collaborative Learning Activity: The Baby Game

Theory or Principle: Genetic instructions determine children's physical characteristics and abilities; and environmental factors influence how these instructions are carried out. The purpose of the Baby Game is to get students thinking about the influence of genetic and environmental factors on the physical and cognitive development of children.

The objective of the game is to birth a healthy baby.

Materials: Each group will need 1 manila folder, colored markers, index cards, playing pieces (boy and girl), scrap paper, and 1 die per group.
<u>NOTE:</u> Party-supply stores are one source for playing pieces (e.g., babies, rattles, baby bottles).

Directions: <u>Creating the materials in two steps</u> – STEP 1 - Students work in groups of 3. Each group creates a game board with 40 squares – one for each week of gestation - see the sample below. Students can include a few "move ahead" or "go back" squares on the game board.

STEP 2 – Students create 20 situation cards. Situation cards are made from blank 3" x 5" index cards. Each card should focus on genetic and environmental factors that affect physical and cognitive development. Use the textbook for ideas of what to write on the cards. Some cards should be positive, and some should be negative. Negative cards subtract from the birth weight and/or I.Q. Positive cards add to those two factors (see samples below).

Sample situation cards:

Mother-to-be realizes that the brain of her fetus is being built, so she takes prescribed vitamin supplements and avoids alcohol and smoking. (+ 2 ounces)	Mother-to-be has one child with Downs Syndrome and refuses genetic counseling. (- 10 I.Q. points)	Mother-to-be is in an abusive relationship and under a lot of stress. (- 4 ounces)

How to Play:

> - Roll the die to determine whether your baby will be a boy or a girl (odd number = girl, even number = boy).
> - Name your child. Write his/her name on a piece of paper and use it to keep track of the health and well-being of your baby. Each baby starts at a standard weight of 7 pounds, with an average I.Q. of 100.
> - Start the game by rolling the die, then moving the number of squares on the die.
> - Pick a situation card, read and discuss it, then add or subtract points from your baby's weight or I.Q.
> - Play until each person's playing piece comes to the end of the board.
> - Discuss and compare the health and well-being of your babies.
> - Talk about both genetic and environmental factors that played a part in the development of the baby.

Chapter 4: Physical Development

Related Picture Book: *Parts* by Tedd Arnold

> *"I just don't know what's going on or why it has to be.*
> *But every day it's something worse. What's happening to me?"*
>
> Arnold, 1997

Synopsis: When the main character in this rollicking, rhyming text loses his first tooth, he panics because he thinks all his teeth will fall out; and then, how will he eat? He tries to make sense of how his body is changing but he can only reason preoperationally, which makes things worse. For example, when he finds hair in his comb, he thinks he going bald; and when he discovers lint in his belly button, he thinks his stuffing is coming out! Finally, his mom, with a *Parenting for Beginners* book tucked under her arm, together with his dad, admit they just forgot to tell him about the physical changes that happen when little boys start to grow up.

Theory or Principle: Physical growth is the product of both nature and nurture. Nature (in the form of genes) instructs bodies to follow a sequence of change according to a timetable. Nurture (in the form of nutrition, loving relationships, and physical activity) blends with nature to create physical growth. The blending of nature and nurture produces dynamic body systems with new and exciting skills, but change can also cause self-consciousness and confusion. Rapid body changes can be scary without explanation to get through those awkward times.

Discussion Questions:
The boy in *Parts* is around 5 years old. He is experiencing many rapid changes and a new awareness of the usual physical changes (e.g., hair loss, belly button lint, peeling skin, a runny nose, a loose tooth, ear wax). Using what you know about physical development in early childhood, create a dialogue to explain these changes to him. Imagine if the character in the story were a little girl. Would you change your explanation? If so, why and how?

Looking ahead to middle childhood and adolescence, what type of information on bodily changes would you prepare to tell the child from the picture book, as he advances in age?

Chapter 4: Physical Development

Related Picture Book: *Love You Forever* by Robert Munsch

"And while she held him, she sang:
I'll love you forever; I'll like you for always,
As long as I'm living, my baby you'll be."

Munsch, 1986

Synopsis: A mother begins a life-long tradition of holding and singing a special lullaby to her new baby boy. Throughout his life, even in adulthood, she makes a point of letting him know how special he is to her and that regardless of what he does, her love is eternal. The strength of her love is tested during the "terrible twos" and the crazy teenage years, but her son recognizes her unconditional love, continuing the family tradition with his own child. The lullaby can be sung to the tune of "On Top of Old Smokey."

Theory or Principle: Bodily changes take place in size, bodily proportions, and neurological structures, throughout childhood. As children grow and develop from infancy, to early and middle childhood, and through to adolescence, successful physical development is related to the practicing of motor skills, healthy eating, opportunities for physical activity, and interaction with peers. Role models and the environment continue to influence children as they explore their growing physical abilities.

Discussion Questions: Parents, teachers, and other professionals can use strategies to promote healthful lifestyles. For example, appropriate indoor and outdoor experiences and provision of appropriate materials can allow children to practice their developing fine- and gross-motor skills. Opportunities to interact with peers through sports and organized play activities promote physical development and set standards for physical activity as a lifestyle. Adolescents need information and support as they go through puberty. Sheila McGraw, the illustrator of *Love You Forever*, presents an accurate illustration for each stage of physical development. Look at the book again and find evidence of experiences, materials, and support that promote healthy physical development as the boy in the story grows to adulthood.

Chapter 4: Physical Development

Collaborative Learning Activity: Food for Thought . . . and Development

Theory or Principle: Early stimulation is essential for optimal brain development. Stimulation and learning are important throughout our lives. The "plasticity" of the brain makes it receptive to the environment and receptive to change. Stimulating and challenging environments exercise the brain, cause dendrites to branch, and cause synapses to grow. In contrast, harmful environments and toxins can cause damage and stunt cognitive growth.

The objective of this activity is to help students understand types of stimulation needed by the brains of children and adolescents. (A sample of a "brain menu" designed for an adolescent follows the activity page.)

Materials: Each student will need a copy of the page, "Food for Thought . . . and Development."

Directions:

1. Identify the stage of development that the menu is designed to address.

2. Decide what entrées and materials will be on the menu.

3. Explain what each entrée is designed to promote (e.g., security, thinking, sensory stimulation, behavior, social skills, or emotional competence).

4. When you have completed your menu, get together with others to discuss it.

5. Why is brain research important for those who work with children and adolescents? What information about the brain will you, as a professional, need? What type of information will you provide to children, adolescents, and their parents?

Feed your brain at Joe's.
We use only the finest, freshest ingredients!

This brain menu is designed for _____

Entrée	Designed to Promote

Feed your brain at Joe's.
We use only the finest, freshest ingredients!

This brain menu is designed for an adolescent.

Entrée	Designed to Promote
art materials like colored pencils, markers, charcoal, and oil paint	creativity, esteem, visual-spatial ability, visual acuity, fine-motor skills
musical instruments and a variety of music like rock, Mozart, and World Beat	auditory skills, mathematical ability (unproven by research), relaxation
mind-challenging board games like crosswords, Sudoku, and word-jumble puzzles	higher-level thinking, concentration, improved working memory, cooperation, relaxation, abstract thinking and reasoning
videos of far-away places and other cultures	social and cultural awareness
basketballs, baseballs, soccer balls, jump ropes	physical strength, coordination, gross-motor skills, cooperation
lessons in yoga and Tai Chi	concentration, relaxation, esteem
books and magazines; writing materials and a journal	mental stimulation, concentration, fine-motor skills
tickets to the symphony, museums, and plays	cultural and social awareness, mental stimulation, relaxation
pamphlets and information on cigarette smoking, and alcohol and drug abuse	safety and understanding of the harmful effects of these substances on the brain

Chapter 5: Family, Culture, and Community

Related Picture Book: *You Are My I Love You* by Maryann Cusimano

"I am your parent; you are my child. I am your quiet place; you are my wild. I am your calm face; you are my giggle. I am your wait; you are my wiggle."

Cusimano, 2001

Synopsis: The relationship between a parent and child can sometimes seem like a tug-of-war with the parent at one end and the child at the other. At other times, that special relationship can be like a beautiful dance with both acting in rhythm, balance, and harmony. These ups, downs, opposites, and balances are portrayed in this beautiful story of a teddy bear parent and child.

Theory or Principle: The interchange that family members have with each other serve as life-long lessons for children in how to respond to authority, how to get along, and what is important to get ready for school. Families, be they conventional or not, lay the foundation for life-long learning and loving.

Discussion Questions:

How did the parent in the book support the child's learning? Did you notice any instances of guided participation? Can you provide examples of how cultures, other than our Western one, lead children to guided participation?

What parenting style was portrayed in the story? What specific examples can you provide from either the story or the illustrations that support your claim?

Families have been called "little schoolhouses." What does this image mean and how was it shown in the story?

The relationship between parent and child is not one-way; socialization of children involves reciprocal influences. Explain how this fact was shown in the story. Share how this situation has occurred in your life as a parent and/or as a child.

Chapter 5: Family, Culture, and Community

Related Picture Book: *I Hate English* by Ellen LeVine

....."and to this day Mei Mei talks in Chinese and in English whenever she wants."
LeVine, 1989

Synopsis: Mei Mei, a young immigrant from Hong Kong, wants to hold on to her language, customs, and ethnic identity. Mei Mei has no use for oral or written English and only sees beauty in Chinese, her native tongue. She attends the Chinatown Learning Center; and there, her life takes a turn. Mei Mei meets a teacher named Nancy who, through her incessant talking about her life in America, helps Mei Mei surface the anger she is feeling about leaving her country, language, and culture. Nancy listens attentively as Mei Mei talks about the customs and celebrations she fears she has lost. That attention helps Mei Mei understand that she can hold on to the memories and customs she cherishes, and still learn English.

Theory or Principle: Ethnicity, culture, family, and gender influence the opportunities of children and adolescents and create their outlook on life. When people move from one environment to another, they must become acculturated to a different place. They often must learn a new language, learn new styles of interaction, new customs, and new beliefs. Acculturation and coping with a new environment is easier for some children than for others. Some groups fit-in easily and readily, while others do not look and act like the dominant culture, resisting loss of language and traditions.

Discussion Questions:
Assimilation, selective adoption, rejection, and bicultural orientation are four forms of acculturation. What form, or combination, of forms of acculturation did Mei Mei fit, and why? What evidence from the story or the illustrations can you provide to support your claim?

If Mei Mei were a boy from Hong Kong instead of a girl, things might have been different. How might a boy be different, and why?

What were some of the challenges Mei Mei faced as a recent immigrant? What coping support did her family and community provide?

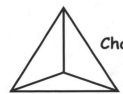

Chapter 5: Family, Culture, and Community

Cradles of Development

Collaborative Learning Activity: Triarama Jigsaw

The cradles of development are important for a happy and healthy childhood. A loving family, exposure to cultural traditions, and a responsive community contribute to children's well-being.

Materials:

- an 8" x 8" piece of paper (this may be colored)
- markers and pencils
- glue and scissors

Directions: There are three steps. Students work in groups of 2 – 4.

Step 1: Investigation. Each group is assigned one cradle of development to investigate. (Keep the distribution equal – one group investigates families, one culture, another community.) Students are to carefully examine what the text says about their area. They need to be able to explain what each cradle is, what it provides, what it affects, and who is involved.

Step 2: Triarama. Each group creates a triarama.

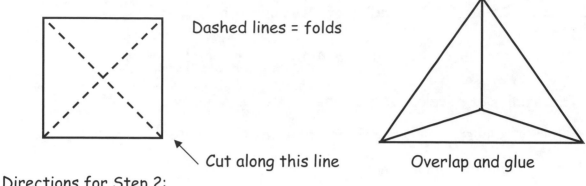

Dashed lines = folds

Cut along this line

Overlap and glue

Directions for Step 2:

1. Fold the top-right corner of the square down to the lower-left corner. Repeat with the opposite corners.

2. Open and cut one fold line to the center of the square *(picture on left)*.

3. Students place what they learned in their investigation on their triarama. Information should be in both pictures and in words.

4. Overlap the two bottom triangles and glue *(picture on the right)*.

Step 3: Jigsaw: After each group of 2 – 4 has created a triarama, have those small groups come together to form larger groups. Each larger group should be comprised of a family group, a culture group, and a community group.

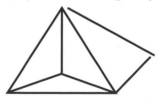

Each group explains their triarama to the others. After the triarama has been discussed, it is placed back-to-back with the others to create a 3-d pyramid shape.

Chapter 6: Cognitive Development: Piaget and Vygotsky

Related Picture Book: *Lilly's Purple Plastic Purse* by Kevin Henkes

> *"Lilly really, really wanted to show everyone.*
> *'Not now,' said Mr. Slinger. 'Wait until recess or Sharing Time.'*
> *But Lilly could not wait."*
>
> Henkes, 1996

Synopsis: Lilly loved school and her teacher, Mr. Slinger, until she got in trouble for not being able to wait to share her purple plastic purse and movie-star sun glasses. Mr. Slinger takes Lilly's precious objects away and she acts like a typical, egocentric preschooler: looking at the world from her own perspective and needs. Lilly writes an angry note, with a mean picture of her teacher, and slips it into his book bag. Lilly realizes that this act is a mistake and, with the help of her parents, she apologizes and makes amends with Mr. Slinger.

Theory or Principle: Jean Piaget spent many years observing and working with children and from this experience, drew inferences about their thinking and reasoning abilities. One of Piaget's most important contributions was his stage theory of cognitive development. Piaget's stage theory is important because it explains how and why children think and reason in qualitatively different ways at different age levels. Piaget's theory of cognitive development has helped educators (and others who work with children) to understand how children think and learn.

Discussion Questions:
According to Piagetian theory, Lilly was in what stage of cognitive development? Provide evidence from the words and pictures in the story to defend your assessment.

Piaget believed that children were active and motivated learners who constructed their own knowledge. What part in the story showed that Lilly was an active and motivated learner? What part in the story showed Lilly using her prior knowledge? What part in the story showed Lilly interacting with others to learn their point of view?

Find an example of Lilly engaged in imaginary play. What would Piaget say about this play and her cognitive growth?

Chapter 6: Cognitive Development: Piaget and Vygotsky

Related Picture Book: *The Three Bears* by Paul Galdone

> *"Then she sat down in the chair of the Little Wee Bear.*
> *It was not too hard. It was not too soft. It was just right."*
>
> Galdone, 1972

Synopsis: In a traditional retelling of this folktale, Goldilocks is an impish little girl with a missing front tooth. The Great Big Bear, the Middle-Sized Bear, and the Little Wee Bear are outraged at her intrusion and in the end, Goldilocks is so frightened that she runs away as fast as she can, never looking behind her.

Theory or Principle: Lev Vygotsky lived at the same time as Piaget. However he gave a very different perspective on cognitive development. To Vygotsky, social interaction and the tools a culture affords are key factors for cognitive growth. Vygotsky did not see learning as stagnant, or at one level, but rather as a dynamic process that occurs between a child and a more capable other, be it an adult or a peer.

In his work, Vygotsky distinguishs between two kinds of abilities that children are likely to possess at any particular point in their development: their actual level of development (what they can do by themselves right now) and their level of potential development (what they can do with assistance and guidance). To Vygotsky, this potential, upper limit is where cognitive growth occurs and the zone where students should be working. The zone of proximal development is the range of tasks a child cannot perform independently but can achieve with guidance and scaffolding.

Discussion Questions:

How is Goldilock's adventure (of finding things that were "just right") like a teacher's quest to find activities in a child's zone of proximal development?

Turn to your neighbor and explain what "zone of proximal development" means.

What will you do to ensure the children and adolescents in your care are working in their zone of proximal development?

Chapter 6: Cognitive Development: Piaget and Vygotsky

Collaborative Learning Activity: Compare and Contrast Piaget and Vygotsky

Theory or Principle: Jean Piaget was curious about children's acquisition of knowledge. As a result of this curiosity, he spent many years observing and working with children. From these experiences, he drew inferences about thinking and reasoning abilities. Some of Piaget's most enduring contributions to psychology include the many concepts he discovered about thinking (e.g., schemes, assimilation, accommodation, and equilibration) and his stage theory of cognitive development.

Lev Vygotsky worked at the same time as Piaget but took a different view of cognitive development, focusing on the role of nurture, especially the way society and culture foster cognitive growth. To Vygotsky, cognitive growth came about through interactions with more-able others and growth developed with the tools (both real and symbolic) that a culture affords.

The objective of this activity is to help students discern the nuances of these two theories of cognitive development.

Materials: One copy of the handout, "Compare and Contrast Piaget and Vygotsky" for each student.

Directions: Students work in groups of 2-3. They place a plus sign (+) if the statement is about the theorist and a minus sign (-) if it is not. Encourage students to discuss their choices and provide a rationale for their choices.

Conclude the session with a discussion of the students' answers. Ask for justification and evidence for items on which students do not agree.

Chapter 6: Cognitive Development: Piaget and Vygotsky

Compare and Contrast Piaget and Vygotsky

Place a plus sign (+) in the box if the principle applies. Place a minus sign (–) if the principle does not apply. Some concepts may apply to both.

	Children actively construct their own knowledge	Higher-order mental processes are mediated by psychological tools that a culture provides	He pioneered the clinical method where an adult presents a task or problem to a child and asks a series of questions about it	He discovered that children do not think like adults	Believed that play provides an arena in which children can practice skills they will need later in life	He is the father of the constructivist movement
Piaget						
Vygotsky						
	Cognitive development improves as adults work with children in their zone of proximal development	Scaffolding, apprenticeship, and peer interaction are contemporary applications of his theory	His focus was on nurture – especially the ways in which social and cultural environments foster cognitive growth	Believed children can perform more advanced tasks when assisted by a competent individual	His theory is referred to as the sociocultural perspective	Equilibration promotes progress toward increasingly more complex levels of thought
Piaget						
Vygotsky						
	Believed cognitive development could only proceed after certain genetically controlled neurological changes occurred	Children engage in egocentric speech with little intent to communicate	Distinguished between a child's actual developmental level and his/her level of potential development or ZPD	Play allows children to stretch themselves cognitively and use their imagination	A child's readiness for a particular task determines the extent to which the task promotes cognitive development	Believed that the challenges in life, not the easy successes, cause cognitive development
Piaget						
Vygotsky						
	Learners are active in social contexts and interactions	Children learn through two complimentary processes of assimilation and accommodation	Children engage in private speech, which is a self-directed tool that aids learning	Children often think in different ways at different ages and these stages are universal to all children worldwide	Cognitive development involves relating new information to prior knowledge	Believed children organize learning from experience into schemes and integrate schemes into operations
Piaget						
Vygotsky						

Chapter 6: Cognitive Development – Compare and Contrast Piaget and Vygotsky

Place a plus sign (+) in the box if the principle applies. Place a minus sign (–) if the principle does not apply. Some concepts may apply to both.

	Children actively construct their own knowledge	Higher-order mental processes are mediated by psychological tools that a culture provides	He pioneered the clinical method where an adult presents a task or problem to a child and asks a series of questions about it	He discovered that children do not think like adults	Believed that play provides an arena in which children can practice skills they will need later in life	He is the father of the constructivist movement
Piaget	+	-	+	+	+	+
Vygotsky	-	+	-	-	+	-
	Cognitive development improves as adults work with children in their zone of proximal development	Scaffolding, apprenticeship, and peer interaction are contemporary applications of his theory	His focus was on nurture – especially the ways in which social and cultural environments foster cognitive growth	Believed children can perform more advanced tasks when assisted by a competent individual	His theory is referred to as the sociocultural perspective	Equilibration promotes progress toward increasingly more complex levels of thought
Piaget	-	-	-	-	-	+
Vygotsky	+	+	+	+	+	-
	Believed cognitive development could only proceed after certain genetically controlled neurological changes occurred	Children engage in egocentric speech with little intent to communicate	Distinguished between a child's actual developmental level and his/her level of potential development or ZPD	Play allows children to stretch themselves cognitively and use their imagination	A child's readiness for a particular task determines the extent to which the task promotes cognitive development	Believed that the challenges in life, not the easy successes, cause cognitive development
Piaget	+	+	-	+	+	-
Vygotsky	-	-	+	+	-	+
	Learners are active in social contexts and interactions	Children learn through two complimentary processes of assimilation and accommodation	Children engage in private speech, which is a self-directed tool that aids learning	Children often think in different ways at different ages and these stages are universal to all children worldwide	Cognitive development involves relating new information to prior knowledge	Believed children organize learning from experience into schemes and integrate schemes into operations
Piaget	-	+	-	+	+	+
Vygotsky	+	-	+	-	-	-

Chapter 7: Cognitive Development: Cognitive Processes

Related Picture Book: Memory Concepts in Various Picture Books

Theory or Principle: Memory is the ability to mentally retain and recall information over a period of time. Memories serve us well when information is organized, accessible, and retrievable; but memories fail us when information is distorted, misattributed, or incomplete. Memory is an abstract concept and can be difficult for students to understand and difficult for teachers to explain.

Materials: Copies of six books: *No, David!, Oh, the Thinks You Can Think!, Fish Is Fish, Knots on a Counting Rope, Willy the Dreamer*, and *Something to Remember Me By.*

Directions: The following picture books are linked to ideas about memory. Specific books can be used to introduce important aspects of memory; or small groups of students can take one book to discover how it connects to learning about memory.

No, David! (Shannon, 1999) is about a little boy who has difficulty paying attention in school. David is a character who can be used as an example of learning to focus attention and self-regulation. David's story can lead to a discussion on attention-getting printed strategies like eye-catching words printed in color, bold print, or italics. You also can inform students of cues teachers use to get attention, such as raising their voice or flickering lights.

Oh, the Thinks You Can Think! (Seuss, 1975) is about thinking up things, thinking about things, and wondering for a long time. It can be used to enlighten students about their tendency to overestimate learning. Seuss informs us about the importance of asking questions, reflection, and deep processing.

Fish Is Fish (Lionni, 1970) is about a fish who assimilates new information into his existing scheme. When the fish hears about cows, he envisions them as large fish with horns and udders. When he hears about birds, he imagines them to be flying fish with wings. The interesting thing about this book is that its illustrations reveal hidden aspects of memory that might otherwise go unseen. Fish was able to assimilate information but needed his friend Frog to reveal to him the distortion of his thinking.

Knots on a Counting Rope (Martin & Archambault, 1987) is about a Navaho boy who asks his grandfather about his birth. The grandfather weaves a fantastic tale and helps his grandson relive memories. The fact that the grandson is blind offers rich insight into intergenerational love and the co-construction of memories.

Willy the Dreamer (Browne, 2000) is about a gorilla who has wild and vivid dreams. The story and magnificent illustrations can be used to help students understand that forming images helps people remember and recall.

Something to Remember Me By: A Story about Love and Legacies (Bosak & McGaw, 2003) is about shared memories and the importance of keeping them in our hearts and minds. The story tells the tale of a young girl's visits to her grandmother's house that always end with a gift and the words "I want to give you something to remember me by." As the grandmother ages and begins to lose her memory, the girl realizes she will remember her grandmother every time she looks in the mirror, because she has her grandmother's smile. This book can help students understand the social construction of memories and how episodic memories are formed.

Chapter 7: Cognitive Development: Cognitive Processes

Related Picture Book: *Wilfred Gordon McDonald Partridge* by Mem Fox

"Wilfred Gordon called on Miss Nancy and gave her each thing one by one. 'What a dear, strange child to bring me all these wonderful things,' thought Miss Nancy. Then she started to remember."

Fox, 1985

Synopsis: A young boy named Wilfred Gordon lives near an old people's home and he sets out to help the elderly Miss Nancy Alison Delacourt find the memories she has lost. To do this task, he places objects in a basket—all have the qualities memories should contain. He puts an egg in the basket because it is warm, he adds a puppet because it makes him laugh, he puts in a medal from his grandfather because it gives him sad memories, and he includes a football because, to Wilfred Gordon, the football is as precious as gold. Wilfred Gordon takes these things to Miss Nancy and gives them to her one by one and, as she touches them, she begins to remember.

Theory or Principle: Metacognition is the term for the knowledge children have about their cognitive processes and intentional use of certain processes to improve learning and memory. As children develop in age, the mental processes they use become increasingly sophisticated and effective. Children develop awareness of the limits of their thinking, strategies to help them remember, and they begin to regulate and direct cognitive resources to learn successfully. But just as memories can be remembered, memories can also be forgotten and fade. If information is processed superficially or not used, it can be difficult to retrieve.

Materials: One copy per student of the strategies handout on the following page.

Directions: Have students work in groups of 2-4 to fill in the strategies. When they are finished, spark a discussion about memory, forgetting, and strategies. Be sure to link these ideas to Wilfred Gordon and Miss Nancy.

Chapter 7: Cognitive Development: Cognitive Processes

Related Picture Book: *Wilfred Gordon McDonald Partridge* by Fox (1985).

The left column contains ideas about remembering and forgetting. Your task is to fill in the right column with strategies to teach to children, to improve memory.

Memory Concepts	Strategies
<u>Putting Information in Memory (encoding)</u> Attention is a mental resource and the beginning of memory. Attention involves tuning out irrelevant information and sustaining attention for a period of time. Students are meaning-makers. They use their prior knowledge to understand the world and to understand what they read. Sometimes this strategy works; but, at other times, using this information causes their thinking to be distorted. There are limits to the number of items one can recall and the amount of time information is kept in consciousness. The mind dual-codes information (both in pictures and in words). Memories are co-constructed with other people. ***Forgetting and Retrieval*** Unused memories can fade over time unless they have been processed deeply and are sometimes brought to mind. Memories can fade over time; but with appropriate retrieval cues, memories can return.	

Chapter 7: Cognitive Development: Cognitive Processes

Collaborative Learning Activity: Information Processing Ladder Book

Theory or Principle: Information processing

The objective of this activity is to help students understand the various components of information processing.

Materials: Each student will need 2 blank pieces of 8 ½" x 11' paper (paper can be light colored), access to markers, and a stapler.

Directions: Have each student create a ladder book.

A. Fold the top of one piece of paper down 2 ½".

B. Take the second piece of paper and fold it down 5 ½".

Place sheet B under the fold of sheet A.

This will create your ladder book (see sample). Staple top of book with two staples.

Begin with the smallest flap. Write information processing on that one.

On the next flap write sensory register and, in the space above, write its code, capacity, and the duration of time information remains. Continue for working memory and long-term memory.

INFORMATION PROCESSING
sensory register
working memory
long-term memory

Chapter 8: Intelligence

Related Picture Book: *Insects Are My Life* by Megan McDonald

*"When I grow up, I'm going to be an entomologist," she
told her mother, "and hatch rare butterflies in my living room."*
McDonald, 1995

Synopsis: Amanda loves bugs and knows a lot about them. She collects them, protects them, acts like them, and thinks like them. Unfortunately, not everyone shares her love, enthusiasm, and obsession for insects and Amanda gets in trouble for her passion both at home and at school. Her mother does not appreciate when Amanda walks like an ant and her teacher does not find the creativity in her sharing and poetry. Furthermore, other children think Amanda is strange. Her brother picks on her, is annoying, and the kids at school laugh and call her names like "bug eyes." Fortunately, her teacher introduces her to Maggie, a girl who loves reptiles as much as Amanda loves insects.

Theory or Principle: No matter how one defines intelligence, some children and adolescents display exceptional talents whereas others show delays. The two ends of the intelligence continuum are commonly known as giftedness and mental retardation. Gifted individuals demonstrate an unusually high ability or aptitude in one or more domains. Many educators view gifted children as having I.Q. scores between 125 or 130. Other experts argue that intelligence has multiple criteria instead of a single point. For example, Howard Gardner (1999) argues there are eight or nine multiple intelligences because people have a variety of independent strengths.

Discussion Questions:
Howard Gardner claims that we have multiple intelligences. What areas of intelligence does Amanda show?

Do you think Amanda may become an underachiever or a social outcast? What evidence can you provide from the story or illustrations to support your thinking?

If Amanda and Maggie were in your classroom, what strategies would you use to help them achieve their full potential? Would your strategies change if they were boys?

Chapter 8: Intelligence

Related Picture Book: *I Miss Franklin P. Shuckles* by Ulana Snihura

"Franklin P. Shuckles can't throw a ball. He has skinny legs and wears funny glasses. Maybe that's why he can't catch either. But he tells the best stories."

Snihura, 1998

Synopsis: Molly Pepper has no one to play with one summer until a new neighbor, Franklin P. Shuckles, moves in. They have a great summer together even though he is different than the other kids. Their friendship is tested when school starts and Molly finds herself embarrassed by her awkward friend. She tries to alienate him in discrete ways but he just doesn't get it. Finally, she resorts to writing him an anonymous note and Franklin silently gives up. Molly finds she misses her gifted but geeky friend and reverses the techniques she used earlier to win back his friendship.

Theory or Principle: Children who are gifted vary in their talents and affinities but as a group they are likely to process information quickly and remember it easily, use effective strategies, and possess advanced reasoning and metacognitive skills. Many gifted individuals set high goals for themselves, seeking out new challenges and mastering them with little guidance. Many gifted students, especially girls, work hard to conceal their gifts and talents for fear of ridicule from their peers.

Discussion Questions:

Using the criteria of processing speed, good memory, advanced reasoning, metacognitive skills, and the use of elaboration, would you consider Franklin P. Shuckles a gifted child? What evidence can you provide from the story or illustrations to explain your view? How does he fit a stereotype of a gifted child?

Proponents of higher education for girls view same-sex high schools as environments where girls can freely meet their potentials in math and science. What do you think about this view? What are some obstacles for girls to meeting their potential in regular public high schools? The idea of same-sex schools has also been conceptualized for boys. Do boys face the same obstacles? Would boys reach a higher potential? Why or why not?

Chapter 8: Intelligence
Collaborative Learning Activity: Take a Culturally Specific Test

Critics of standardized intelligence and achievement tests claim that these instruments are culturally biased. They claim that the developers of these tests favor items that reflect their primarily white, middle-class, ethnocentric backgrounds. To appreciate what it must be like to take a test that discriminates against people from a different background, try to answer the multiple-choice questions that follow. Keep in mind, that if they seem confusing, hard to answer, or misleading, then you are beginning to understand how test questions are inexorably entwined with culture.

The questions were generated from common knowledge among Canadians. Imagine what it would be like if you did not speak the same language as these people, eh?!

1. What is the definition of a skidoo? (a) the popular refrain of a song (b) a motorized snow vehicle (c) tracks behind a pair of skis (d) leaving a room very quickly	2. A friend brings you back a toonie from Canada. What do you do with it? (a) put it on your head (b) deposit it in the bank (c) share it with him (d) refer to it in your next writing assignment
3. A serviette is known across the country as (a) a tray at a fast-food restaurant (b) a female waitress (c) a paper napkin (d) a small token of approval after a meal	4. Your buddy comes back from Canada sporting a Molson Muscle. You are surprised because (a) his car goes a lot faster (b) he obviously has been working out (c) he has gained a lot of weight (d) his shirts are missing sleeves
5. Poutine is (a) French fries covered with gravy and cheese curds (b) the French word for being sad (c) French words under the English equivalent on road signs (d) the French way to dismiss people who are not bilingual	6. If you are reminded to include a postal code, you would (a) go crazy at the request (b) use letters and numbers to speed mail delivery (c) add the 2-letter provincial abbreviation (d) add an additional 5 cents postage to defray the cost of speedy delivery
7. Gyprock is (a) a phony diamond ring (b) an interior wall board (c) a stone with a hollow interior (d) an English country garden	8. There are many Anglophones in Canada. That would be: (a) the Canadian equivalent of a saxophone (b) a metric protractor (c) a telephone with a rotary dial (d) a person whose first language is English

Chapter 8: Intelligence

Collaborative Learning Activity: Take a Culturally Specific Test

Correct answers and explanations are as follows.

---

1 – B. Skidoo is a brand name of a snowmobile popular in Canada.

2 – B. One-dollar coins have a picture of a loon on the front. Canadians started called them "loonies." When a two-dollar coin was introduced, the popular term became "toonie." A toonie has a picture of a polar bear on the front. Both coins have a portrait of Queen Elizabeth II on the back.

3 – C. A serviette is a paper napkin.

4 – C. Molson Brewery produces a beer popular with Canadians. A beer belly is jokingly referred to as a "Molson Muscle."

5 – A. More popular in the east than the west, poutine is a fast-food favorite – yum!

6 – B. A postal code is the equivalent of a U.S. zip code. Canadians use a combination of letters and number (versus numbers only). For example, mail directed to Fort Saskatchewan, in the province of Alberta, would go to T8L 4J5.

7 – B. Gyprock is an interior wall board made from gypsum. A U.S. equivalent would be sheet rock.

8 – D. An Anglophone is a person whose first language is English. Canada has two official languages: English and French. A person whose first language is French is referred to as a Francophone.

Chapter 9: Language Development

Related Picture Book: *Hooway for Wodney Wat* by Helen Lester

> *"All this teasing day in and day out made Wodney the shyest rodent*
> *in his elementary school. His squeak could barely be heard in class.*
> *He gnawed his lunch alone."*

Lester, 1999

Synopsis: Wodney Wat's real name is *Rodney Rat*, but he has difficulty pronouncing his *r*'s. This difficulty, of course, makes him the victim of much teasing and so Rodney becomes the shyest rodent in school. Add to the mix the biggest, meanest bully in the form of Camilla Capybara and things just get worse! When it is Rodney's turn to lead the class in "Simon Says" he knows Camilla will discover his speech impediment and join his list of tormentors. However, by the end of the game, Rodney reveals Camilla's weak spots and uses them to everyone's advantage. The class gets rid of Camilla; Rodney becomes the hero of the school.

Theory or Principle: Many children develop normally in all respects except for speech and language. Children with speech and communication disorders have difficulty with expressive and/or receptive language that significantly interferes with their social interactions and their performance in school.

Discussion Questions: Speech and communication disorders take several forms. A child can have difficulty with receptive language, articulation, fluency, syntax, semantics, and pragmatics, or a combination of several problems. What type of disorder did Rodney Rat have? Did Rodney display age-appropriate language? What evidence can you provide from the story for your answer?

What personal and social problems did Rodney's language difficulties cause for him in the classroom and outside?

Although specialists work with children who have impaired communication skills, others (teachers, parents, and counselors) also lend their support. If you were working with Rodney, what are some of the things you would do to encourage his language and cognitive skills?

Chapter 9: Language Development

Related Picture Book: *Marianthe's Story* by Aliki

"Slowly, like clouds lifting, things became clearer.
Sticks and chicken feet became letters.
Sputters and coughs became words and the words had meanings."

Aliki, 1998

Synopsis: One side of this book is called *Painted Words*. It tells of a young girl who enters an English-speaking classroom buoyed by her mother's words that a smile is the same in any language. She is a little afraid, but not enough to cry. Her classmates notice that she communicates with them through her paintings and eventually, Marianthe shares her life and feelings page-by-painted page. The book flips over to share *Spoken Memories* – the story of Marianthe's life in a poor village before moving to her new country.

Theory or Principle: Bilingualism is the ability to speak two languages. Acquiring proficiency in a second language is easier during childhood. It is possible (but not to the point of native fluency) before puberty. It is noticeably more difficult after puberty. Being bilingual helps children develop metalinguistic sophistication and advanced cognitive skills. Besides cognitive benefits, being bilingual has cultural and personal advantages. Bilingual individuals have the benefit of learning their culture's oral history, of showing respect to elders who speak only their native tongue, and of maintaining personal relationships with important people in their lives.

Discussion Questions:

There is nothing in the text or illustrations to indicate where Marianthe came from. Does that make any difference? Why or why not?

What cultural differences were evident in Marianthe's sociolinguistic behaviors?

Describe the pros and cons of immersion and bilingual education. Which would be a better fit for Marianthe, and why?

Chapter 9: Language Development

Collaborative Learning Activity:
Links in the Chain—Appreciating Black English Vernacular

Related Picture Book: *'Twas the Night B'fore Christmas* by Melodye Rosales

> *"'Twas the night b'fore Christmas, when all 'round the house,*
> *not a critter was stirrin', not even a mouse.*
> *The stockin's were laid by the chimney wit' care,*
> *for the chil'ren hoped Santy Claus soon would be there."*
>
> Rosales, 1996

Synopsis: This classic poem is retold in African American English and illustrated from this perspective.

Theory or Principle: Sociolinguistic conventions, use of figurative language, and narrative styles differ from one ethnic group to another. Additionally, children from different ethnic and cultural backgrounds might use a varied form of English that is different from Standard English, or different from the typical language spoken at school. The most widely studied dialect is African American English, or Black English Vernacular. This dialect has its own unique pronunciations, idioms, and grammatical constructions.

Materials: Copies of *'Twas the Night B'fore Christmas* (one copy per group), copy of the Links in the Chain activity page that follows, and tape.

Directions: Cut a copy of the Links in the Chain activity page into strips and place one strip inside copies of Rosales's *'Twas the Night B'fore Christmas*. Divide students into eight groups. Each group reads the story and answers the problem strip inside their copy of the book.

After groups finish their strip, have them share their findings and place the strip as a link in the chain. When the chain is completed, finish the session by considering the following scenario. Some individuals perceive people in a lesser light if those people speak a dialect other than Standard English. However, many teachers have found ways to encourage the use of Standard English while allowing children the time and space to use their unique dialect. Provide examples of how this method might be accomplished.

Chapter 9: Language Development
Links in the Chain - Appreciating Black English Vernacular

Collaborative Activity based on '*Twas the Night B'fore Christmas* (Rosales, 1996)

1. African American English, or Black English Vernacular, has its own unique pronunciations, idioms, and grammatical constructions. Provide examples of these from the book.

2. H. L. Smith (1998) noted that many African American communities make heavy use of figurative language. Provide examples of this from the book.

3. "Playing the dozens" is a form of creative word play involving teasing through exaggerated insults. Find an example of "playing the dozens" in this book.

4. Exaggeration (hyperbole) has been noted as evident in African American storytelling. Find an example of exaggeration in this story.

5. African American dialect is a complex form of language with predictable idioms and grammatical rules. Find examples of a predictable grammatical rule.

6. Semantic bootstrapping is using one's knowledge of word meanings to figure out how language is structured and categorized (syntax). Identify an example of when you used what you know about meaning, to understand the way the words were presented in this book.

7. Make a case for Rosales's version of *Twas the Night B'fore Christmas* as an example of bilingualism.

8. How do the language and illustrations in the book provide examples of sociocultural theory?

Chapter 10: Development in the Content Domains

Related Picture Book: *Froggy Bakes a Cake* by Jonathon London

> *"Then he dumped all the goopy cake batter into a cake pan . . .*
> *and shoved the cake into the oven. And he sang:*
> *Oogelly boogelly burbly bake. I make and I bake and I wait for the cake."*
> London, 2000

Synopsis: In this continuing adventure in the series, Froggy decides to bake a cake for his mother all by himself and, as usual, finds himself in a situation where his face is more red than green. His antics are celebrated in a delightful use of phonics: everywhere he goes is with a *flop, flop, flop*; and his father stretches out his son's names in syllables – *Frrooggyy* – to which his son always replies by dividing his answer into phonemes – *wha – a- a- af?*

Theory or Principle: Phonological awareness is not the same as phonics. Phonological awareness is the understanding that spoken words are made up of separate units of sound, blended together when words are pronounced. It can also be thought of as the skill of hearing and pronouncing the separate sounds in words. Phonological awareness is an auditory skill that children need to develop before they begin to match symbols to letter sounds.

Discussion Questions:
Phonological awareness includes abilities such as hearing the specific syllables within words, dividing words into discrete word sounds, blending phonemes into words, and identifying words that rhyme. What elements of phonological awareness are modeled in this book?

Why do silly rhyme words appeal to young children? How does this idea promote phonological awareness?

It is more effective to promote phonological awareness within the context of lively, enjoyable listening, than with reading and spelling activities. What strategies will you use to promote phonemic awareness in the children you will work with?

How could you use this book to help emerging readers begin the process of understanding how written words work?

Chapter 10: Development in the Content Domains

Related Picture Book: *Thank You, Mr. Falker* by Patricia Polacco

"But, little one, don't you understand, you don't see letters or numbers the way other people do. And you've gotten through school all this time, and fooled many, many good teachers! That took cunning, and smartness, and such, such bravery."

Polacco, 1998

Synopsis: Despite growing up in a family that honored reading, Tricia finds it next-to-impossible to learn how to read. She compensates for her disability the best she can until the torment of classmates brings her to a breaking point. Fortunately, Mr. Falker (a kind and compassionate teacher) and Miss Plessy (a reading specialist) intervene and use special methods to help Tricia overcome her learning problems. This story is a true one – the author's own – and a tribute to the difference a caring person can make in one child's life.

Theory or Principle: There is much diversity in reading development. Some children easily pick-up letter names and sounds and are reading before they enter school. Others struggle with phonological awareness, have trouble identifying visual stimuli quickly, and find it impossible to automatize the connection between print and meaning. In its extreme form, this struggle with print is known as dyslexia, a disability that often has biological roots. During the past decade, there has been much progress made in understanding children with dyslexia, their challenges, and their strengths. Engaging children in meaningful activities, while emphasizing basic reading skills (with explicit instruction to strategies and concepts they have missed), facilitates reading development for children who struggle with print.

Discussion Questions:
Trisha grew up in a family that honored literacy and encouraged the children to become readers. Using the story and pictures in the book, explain the types of activities Trisha's family used to encourage her literacy development.

If Trisha came from a different socioeconomic background, were a boy instead of a girl, or came from a different ethnic and cultural group. how might development of her literacy skills and been different? What would each group emphasize and what would this mean to her?

What are some of the characteristics of dyslexia that Trish displayed? If Trisha were a student in your classroom, what strategies and materials would you use to promote her literacy development?

One way to help struggling readers is early identification. Use the story and its illustrations to explain early signs of Trisha's difficulties. How would you identify and remediate reading challenges in a young child?

Carefully examine the illustrations and describe Trisha's self-esteem and self-concept as she went through school.

Trisha, like many students with special needs, was a victim of bullying. Explain (using specific quotes from the story) how Mr. Falker helped Trisha gain empowerment. What strategies might you have tried?

Chapter 10: Development in the Content Domains

Collaborative Activity: Math Curse Brochure

Related Picture Book: *Math Curse* by Jon Scieszka and Lane Smith

> *"Math is just a total problem. Mrs. Fibonacci says*
> *there are many ways to count."*
>
> Scieszka & Smith, 1995

Synopsis: The day after her teacher announces, "You know, you can think of almost everything as a math problem," the child in the story is afflicted with the "math curse" that leads her to begin looking at the world through a mathematical lens. English class becomes word problems, lunchtime brings fraction problems, and the bus ride home from school brings problems of distance and measurement. The story helps us understand the importance and practical use of math in our lives every day.

Theory or Principle: Mathematics is a cluster of domains (such as arithmetic, algebra, and geometry). To become proficient in mathematics, children need to develop knowledge and skills. The best way to promote proficiency of mathematics is through connections to real life rather than rote memorization.

Materials: A piece of 8 ½" x 11" paper and markers for each person.

Directions: Advertisers use brochures to sell exotic trips or unique products. The purpose of this activity is for students to sell the usefulness and practicality of math to children and adolescents.

Read *Math Curse* to students; then:

1. Present the following ideas about mathematics. Have students provide their viewpoints.
   - mathematics is a collection of meaningless procedures that must be memorized and recalled
   - math problems have one (and only one) correct answer
   - one should be able to solve a math problem quickly or one will not be able to solve it at all

2. How did the girl in the story dispel these mathematics myths?

3. The story teaches an important lesson about mathematics in our lives. What is this lesson? Why is it so valuable to help children understand this lesson?

After this discussion, have students create a brochure for mathematics by folding their paper in three sections.

Math is
important
in my
life
because...

The brochure should emphasize the importance and practicality of math in everyday life. It should also contain ideas about where and how mathematics is used every day. Encourage students to use both pictures and words in their brochure.

To wrap up, have students get into groups and share their brochures. Also have them discuss specific strategies they will use to help children and adolescents understand the usefulness and practicality of mathematics.

Chapter 11: Emotional Development

Related Picture Book: *Owen* by Kevin Henkes

> *"Owen had a fuzzy yellow blanket…*
> *He loved it with all his heart."*

Henkes, 1993

Synopsis: Owen counts on Fuzzy, the yellow blanket he has had since he was a baby, to help him deal with stressful situations like "nail clippings and haircuts." Mrs. Tweezers, a well-meaning neighbor, advises Owen's parents that it is time for him to be a big boy and get rid of his security blanket. However, Owen doesn't give up easily. Tried-and-true detachment methods (like the Blanket Fairy and vinegar on a corner) fail to squelch his attachment to Fuzzy. Being a sensitive caregiver, Owen's mother comes up with the perfect plan. She cuts Fuzzy into little handkerchiefs and this plan allows Owen to continue to keep his blanket with him and benefit from the security it provides. Owen begins school with his not-so-fuzzy handkerchief; and Mrs. Tweezers, who has a handkerchief of her own, does not say a thing.

Theory or Principle: Attachments are enduring emotional ties that link one person to another. To infants, attachments are necessary for their survival and influence cognitive, emotional, and social growth. Children with secure attachments tend to be self-confident, do well in school, and are liked by their teachers and peers.

Infants have ways to become attached to their important caregivers and keep them nearby. They smile and cry, and cling and crawl to them. Attachment is universal; and parents, like infants, are biologically predisposed to be attuned to their baby's signals and to care for their needs. Secure attachments depend on caregivers who are perceptive, responsive, and nurturing. Sensitive caregivers take cues from their infants and allow them to influence the pace and direction of their interactions. There are individual differences in attachment styles; further, attachments change, broaden, and develop over time. For example, even though the world of middle-schoolers is expanding, such children still depend and need attachments with family members and other caregivers. If adults are not there for middle school children, they may become angry, aggressive, or physically ill. Adolescent attachment relations change as young people become less emotionally dependent and assert their independence. However, no matter how old we grow, most of us still need our parents and caregivers, and we remain attached to them.

Discussion Questions: Imagine how Owen and his mother would act if they were placed in the Strange Situation. What would Owen do when his mother left the room and returned? How would Owen's mother act when she returned to the room and was reunited with him? Using Ainsworth's (1978) classifications, determine if Owen would be classified as secure, insecure-avoidant, insecure-resistant, or disorganized and disoriented.

In the story, ideas to cure Owen of his attachment and need for Fuzzy included ideas like the Blanket Fairy, being a big boy, and the vinegar. Investigate these notions in terms of gender, culture, and individual differences. Then research how various cultures differ in infant-caregiver relations.

Why do you think children form attachments with inanimate objects (like security blankets or teddy bears)?

Carefully examine the illustrations in the text and use them as evidence to explain ways that Owen's mother and father contributed to his attachment.

Imagine what Owen will be like cognitively, emotionally, and socially as he grows and develops. Do you think Owen's strong attachment with his parents will continue as he enters middle childhood and adolescence? Why or why not? What evidence from the story or illustrations can you provide?

How will you (as an educator, caregiver, specialist, administrator, mental health professional, or youth service or health-care provider) ensure the attachment of the children and adolescents with whom you are working?

Reflect upon the attachment relations in your own life.

Chapter 11: Emotional Development

Related Picture Book: *How Are You Peeling? Foods with Moods* by Saxton Freymann and Joost Elffers

"When how you feel is understood, you have a friend, and that feels good."
Freymann & Elffers, 1999

Synopsis: The creators of this book used an ordinary X-acto™ knife and natural materials, such as black-eyed peas and beet-juice coloring, to create a range of emotions on common fruits and vegetables. Along with the illustrations, rhyming text draws comparisons among emotions and invites the reader to talk about emotions. The book opens dialogue about sadness, anger, fear, and embarrassment. The artwork is superb and the feelings are appropriate for discussion at all ages.

Theory or Principle: Emotions (or *affect*) are both physiological and psychological feelings that children have in response to events in their world. Emotions are relevant to children because emotions focus their attention, energize their bodies, and organize their thinking. Emotional expression unfolds with age and experience and is influenced by group membership—by gender, family, culture, and socioeconomic status. Four common emotional-behavioral disorders are depression, suicide, anxiety, and conduct problems.

Discussion Questions: If the author of this book provided no words, what physical cues in the illustrations could you use to determine the emotions portrayed in the story?

How Are You Peeling? portrays a range of both positive and negative emotions on fruit and vegetables. In real life and with real children, the development of emotions changes from infancy to adolescence. What are some of the characteristics of emotional development?

Why is it so important for children to learn how to regulate their emotions? What is the impact of emotional regulation on learning?

What biological, psychological, and/or environmental factors lead to emotional problems in children and adolescents?

Chapter 11: Emotional Development

Collaborative Learning Activity: Emotional Charades

Related Picture Book: *When Sophie Gets Angry—Really, Really Angry* by Molly Bang

"She kicks. She screams. She wants to smash the world to smithereens."
Bang, 1999

Synopsis: Having to share her gorilla with her sister sets Sophie on an emotional roller coaster. Finally, through the comfort found in releasing her feelings verbally, physically, and taking time for herself, she returns home where it smells and feels good. Everyone is glad she is home and everything is back together again.

Theory or Principle: Emotions are feelings, both physiological and psychological, in response to events that are personally relevant. As children develop, their emotions change and they also change the way they cope with their emotions. Infants begin life with a few basic emotions and, as children grow, their repertoire of emotions expands to include self-conscious ones. Infants do little to regulate their emotions, whereas older children develop strategies to cope with the powerful emotions they sometimes feel.

To introduce this activity, read *When Sophie Gets Angry—Really, Really Angry* by Molly Bang (1999). As you read the story, point out how Molly Bang uses color, facial expressions, body language, and varied print to express emotions. Then tell the students they are going to participate in an activity where they will express their emotions with their bodies, voices, faces, and movement.

Materials: Copy the list of emotions on the descriptors page and cut the list into strips. Place the strips in a container.

Directions: There are two rounds.
Round 1:
1. Students sit in a circle.
2. One student selects a strip out of the container and acts out that emotion.
3. Others try to guess the emotion.

Round 2:

1. After the first round, make the activity a bit more complex by assigning an age level. For example, the student in the center must act like an infant who is fearful. Another must act like an adolescent who is apprehensive.

2. Students try to guess the emotion and identify the age level.

Discussion Questions: When the activity is over, ask students to explain the specific cues (voice, body posture, facial expressions) they used to understand the emotion being expressed.

Then return to the book and discuss Sophie's emotions and the things she did to regulate her feelings in appropriate ways. After this discussion, explain that emotional literacy is the ability to read and understand one's own emotions and the emotions of others. Emotional literacy is an important skill but one many children (especially boys) fail to develop. Ask students to work into small groups and devise a plan they can use to help the children they work with to develop their emotional literacy.

1. How can they help children understand and label the emotions that they feel?

2. Brainstorm a list of constructive things children can do when difficult or negative emotions arise. Then have students think of ways to set up the environment to allow these forms of expression.

Chapter 11: Emotional Development
Descriptors for Emotional Charades
Related Picture Book: *When Sophie Gets Angry—Really, Really Angry* (Bang, 1999)

FEAR
SADNESS
DISGUST
EMBARRASSMENT
ANGER
AGONY
APPREHENSION
PRIDE
SURPRISE
CONTEMPT
JOY
ANNOYANCE
SHAME
WORRY

Chapter 11: Emotional Development

Collaborative Learning Activity:
A Life-Span Approach to Personal and Emotional Development

Theory or Principle: Erik Erikson (1959) outlined eight developmental periods (psychosocial stages) of personal and emotional growth. Erikson proposed that people face developmental challenges, and the way that people resolve these crises contributes to psychological and social well-being.

Materials: Overhead transparency machine, eight transparencies, and transparency markers.

Directions: Divide students into eight groups. Randomly assign each group one of Erikson's proposed stages of psychosocial personal and emotional development. Each group will have an overhead transparency and permanent markers. The task for each group is to draw pictures representing opposite ends of emotional development (at that stage of life). Each group will present its drawings to the rest of the class, define the conflict at each life stage, and talk about a balanced medium.

Activity Samples:

Chapter 12: Development of Self and Social Understanding

Related Picture Book: *The Sissy Duckling* by Harvey Fierstein and Henry Cole

*"Yes, Elmer was one happy duckling doing all the things he loved to do.
Unfortunately, there wasn't a single other little boy duckling who liked
to do any of the stuff that Elmer did. Not one."*

Fierstein and Cole, 2002

Synopsis: Elmer is happy doing the things he loves best: baking, performing, and playing with girls. His non-conformity to traditional gender stereotypes gets him in trouble with his father and the other boys who cannot understand such a sissy duckling. Banished from his family, Elmer sets off in search of a place where he can be himself. Fortunately, finding his inner strength and sense of self leads Elmer to save the day.

Theory or Principle: Feelings, beliefs, and judgments about one's self are known collectively as a "sense of self." This sense of self goes by several terms: self-concept (Who am I?) or self-esteem and self-worth (How good am I?). A sense of self helps children and adolescents make sense of and organize the things that happen to them and behave in certain ways. Both environmental and biological factors influence the development of a sense of self.

Discussion Questions:
Children and adolescents develop a sense of self based on their past behaviors and performance. How was this idea shown in the story?

Other people influence our sense of self by communicating, through both words and behaviors, messages to us about our strengths, weaknesses, and overall worth. Using the illustrations and story, explain what ideas were communicated to Elmer about his sense of self. How were these ideas communicated?

One important component of children's sense of self is the gender schema they create. Gender schemas help children understand what males and females are like and the appropriate things that each gender does. Describe the gender schema Elmer had and contrast it to the gender schema his father and his peers possessed.

In many ways, Elmer provides us with a good example of an androgynous youngster. Explain what androgyny means and provide examples from the story and the illustrations to back up this claim.

How could you use Elmer's story to enhance children's sense of self?

Chapter 12: Development of Self and Social Understanding

Related Picture Book: *Once There Were Giants* by Martin Waddell

"When I got to sixth grade I had lots of fun.
I got big and strong and punched my brother John.
He is the one with the sore nose. The one with the black eye is me."

Waddell, 1989

Synopsis: This story takes the reader through the life of a child from birth to the birth of her own child. The story and illustrations reveal how adults are giants to a child: their actions seem larger than life. The book is filled with autobiographical memories revealed in both pictures and in words.

Theory or Principle: One important aspect of a sense of self is an autobiographical self (a mental history of the important events and people in one's life). This expanding personal history becomes a part of how children and adolescents conceptualize themselves. The more adults discuss and reminisce with children, the more memories children will retain.

Discussion Questions:
As children's cognitive development expands, they begin to build an autobiographical self. Turn to the person on your left and explain what this concept means.

This book is, in essence, is a girl's autobiographical self. If you were to write a story of your autobiographical self, what characters and events would it contain?

Individuals who work with children help them build an autobiographical self. Activities, special occasions, words spoken, and interactions become part of a child's memory. In what ways will you foster a positive sense of self in the children and adolescents in your life? What special memories do you hope they will form about you?

Individuals who work with children help them remember special memories by talking and reminiscing with them. How will you include reminiscing in your interaction with children and adolescents?

Chapter 12: Development of Self and Social Understanding

Related Picture Book: *Stand Tall, Molly Lou Melon* by Patty Lovell

"Molly Lou Melon was often fumble fingered. She didn't mind. Her grandma had told her, 'Believe in yourself and the world will believe in you too.' "

Lovell, 2001

Synopsis: Molly Lou Melon had buck teeth that stuck out so far, she could stack pennies on them and that was just the beginning of her unattractive physical characteristics! However, Molly Lou had a grandma who loved her just the way she was and helped her to see her own special abilities, inner beauty, and strength. When Molly Lou moves away from her supportive grandmother and enters a new school, her self-esteem becomes challenged by Ronald Durkin, a bully who confronts and torments her. With the voice of her grandmother backing her and all the courage she can muster, Molly Lou beats Ronald at his own game to gain the respect she deserves. In the end Molly Lou thanks her grandmother in a letter that says everything her grandmother had told her was exactly right!

Theory or Principle: As children develop, they begin to understand their abilities, weaknesses, and strengths. Self-concept includes beliefs about one's self, one's characteristics, and abilities. Self-esteem is the feeling one develops about one's capacity and self-worth. Self-efficacy is the belief that one is capable of meeting challenges and reaching goals in a particular domain. These three concepts can be challenged when children enter formal education and as they venture into the world.

Resiliency is the tendency of some children and adolescents to thrive despite harmful and cruel conditions. Many young people beat the odds even though they suffer from maltreatment by their parents or their peers, and even though they exist in harsh environmental conditions like poverty or neglect. Self-concept, self-worth, and self-efficacy can be challenged and damaged by cruelty or unreasonable expectations. The key to resiliency is having one or more individuals in one's life to trust and turn to in difficult times. Besides parents, sources of resiliency include out-of-home caregivers, grandparents, and teachers.

Discussion Questions:

Describe Molly Lou's self-concept, self-esteem, and self-efficacy at the beginning of the story. Describe how each of these qualities changed after she moves to a new school. Is it typical for these to change when children encounter new situations and challenges?

How did Molly Lou Melon display resiliency?

Schools are taking an active stance to prevent bullying. How did Molly Lou deal effectively with the bullying tactics of Ronald Durkin? Do you think that Molly Lou bullied Ronald? Why or why not?

How might peer mediation have been used in this situation?

Parents are absent in this story. Why do you think the author chose to present the grandmother as Molly Lou's source of resiliency? What implications does this factor have for you, as someone who will work with children? What will you do to foster resiliency in the children with whom you will work?

Chapter 13: Development of Motivation and Self-Regulation

Related Picture Book: *David Gets in Trouble* by David Shannon

"When David gets in trouble he always says . . . no, it's not my fault."

Shannon, 2002

Synopsis: David is a little boy who lacks impulse control and knows every excuse in the book as to why. "It's not my fault" or "It's just an accident" are mantras he has learned to excuse his behaviors. However, in the end, David makes an important discovery—it was him making those choices, and he is sorry that he did.

Theory or Principle: Children gain self-regulation as they experience their world and social expectations. The development of self-regulation can be seen as individuals move from external controls and reminders to internal dialogue and control. Parents and teachers can foster children's self-regulation with warm, supportive relationships and consistent, fair discipline.

Discussion Questions: Self-regulation includes impulse control, emotional regulation, self-socialization, goal setting, gratification delay, self-motivation, and self-regulated learning. Carefully examine the story and illustrations to see which of these factors of self-regulation David possessed or lacked.

Self-regulation depends on growing cognitive abilities, such as anticipating consequences, and inhibiting thoughts and behaviors. Self-regulation includes sustaining thoughts in one's working memory to think about what behaviors should and should not be performed. Think a moment about these developmental trends in self-regulation; which ones did David possess or lack? Provide evidence for your answer from the story and illustrations.

At the end of the story, David made a big break-through in his understanding of self-regulation, because he realized that he was making choices and using excuses. To this new insight, David's mother replies that she loves him. What type of behaviors and words might David's parents have said and done to encourage his new understanding of his behavior and self-regulation? As an individual who wants to work with children, what type of things will you do and say to encourage the self-regulation of children in your care?

Chapter 13: Development of Motivation and Self-Regulation

Related Picture Book: *Pink and Say* by Patricia Polacco

"'I don't want to go back,' I blurted out. . . 'You don't understand. I took up and run away from my unit. I was hit when I was runnin'.' I sobbed so hard my ribs hurt. 'I'm a coward and a deserter.'"

Polacco, 1994

Synopsis: This story is set during the Civil War, a time when the morals and principles of many young men were challenged when they were called to fight. It begins when a young boy named Pinkus (Pink) finds Sheldon Curtis (Say) injured in battle. Pink takes Say home to his mother, Moe Moe Bay, who nurses him back to health, both physically and psychologically. Say had deserted his unit and was being tormented by sadness and guilt. With Moe Moe Bay's love and understanding, Say begins to understand and cope with what he had done. But harboring Union soldiers put Moe Moe bay in danger and marauders murder her simply because she is black. The boys are also faced with danger when they get taken to a Confederate prison camp. The boys get separated and Pink dies by hanging.

Theory or Principle: Morality is a set of standards about right and wrong. Moral individuals are honest, compassionate, respectful, and honest. Immoral behaviors include actions that are unfair or cruel, and actions that cause emotional, physical, or psychological harm. Families, schools, and relationships strongly influence the development of moral actions in young people. Life experiences, and the era in which children grow up, can also influence the moral code by which they live.

Theorists have approached the study of moral development from three very different views. Some focus on socialization and investigate how morals hold groups together to survive. Others focus on cognition and view moral thinking as constructed by the individual and linked to changing cognitive skills. A third view focuses on the role that emotions play. We become moral because we have emotions and can empathize with others. While no sole view explains the complexity of moral development, each contributes to our understanding.

One of the most famous cognitive, or constructivist, views of moral development is Lawrence Kohlberg's theory. Kohlberg (1983) believed moral development is characterized by a series of stages. His proposed three levels (with six stages)

move moral reasoning from the concrete level to the abstract understanding of right and wrong.

Discussion Questions:
There are many moral dilemmas posed in the story. For example, when Pink finds Say, he must decide if he will help him or let him die. Moe Moe Bay, a black slave, was faced with the dilemma of deciding if she would help Say, a Union solider. Say had faced the dilemma of fighting in battle and had decided to run.

Carefully go through the story and find moral dilemmas. Use Kohlberg's theory to determine the level of reasoning being used by each character in the dilemmas you found.

Examine the actions of Pink, Say, Moe Moe Bay, the marauders, and the prison guards through the various theoretical lenses. How were their morals influenced by socialization, cognition, and emotions?

Pink and Say were likely in the late adolescent stage, yet they faced many moral issues above their reasoning skills. Do you think young people today face a similar situation? If so, what are some examples? If not, why?

Carol Gilligan (1982) has challenged Kohlberg's views. Gilligan believes that females do not base their moral judgments on issues of fairness but rather on interpersonal relationships and concern. What are some moral dilemmas that young girls face in today's world? What are moral dilemmas in today's world that young boys face? Do you think gender influences how each group reacts? Do you believe culture influences different standards and perceptions of right or wrong?

How will you promote the moral development of the children in your care?

Chapter 13: Development of Motivation and Self-Regulation

Related Picture Book: *Willy the Wizard* by Anthony Browne

"Willy was sure his cleats were magic."

Browne, 2003

Synopsis: Willy loves soccer and wants to become a soccer star but he does not have a pair of cleats. That is until one day when a magic stranger gives him a pair. Willy makes the team, practices, shoots and dribbles, and gets better. Willy attributes his success to the cleats and is convinced that his cleats are magic.

Unfortunately, on the day of the big game, Willy forgets his cleats and has to play with a loaned pair. The ending leaves Willy (and the reader) wondering about the true nature of his cleats. Did they cause Willy to succeed or was it something else?

Theory or Principle: Attributions are the various explanations that people give for their success and failure, or the success and failure of others. Attributions contain beliefs about aptitude or ability, effort, others, luck, mood, illness, and task difficulty. Attributions differ in three ways: their location, their stability, and their controllability. Attributions are self-constructed perceptions and do not always reflect reality. Fortunately, adults who work with children can help them build positive attributions by helping them see that success and failure are controllable and internal.

Materials: A copy of the following page about analyzing attributions, one per student.

Discussion Questions: Have students work together to determine the locus, stability, and controllability of the following attributions.

Chapter 13: Development of Motivation and Self-Regulation

Analyzing Attributions: Think about Willy from *Willy the Wizard* (Browne, 2003) and analyze each of the following attributions with respect to locus, stability, and controllability. The first one has been completed for you.

After a success Willy says...I was successful because...

	Locus: (internal or external)	Stability: (stable or unstable)	Controllability: (controllable or uncontrollable)
"I'll win every game because I have talent."	I	S	U
"I scored because I was wearing my cleats."			
"Soccer is easy!"			
"Coach gave me some good plays and I used them to win."			
"I won because I had beginner's luck."			
"The stranger helped me win."			
"My team's really good because we practice."			
"My cleats are magic."			
"I am a Wizard because I studied the plays coach gave me."			
"My team tried super hard and will try hard again next time."			

After a failure Willy says...I failed because...

	Locus: (internal or external)	Stability: (stable or unstable)	Controllability: (controllable or uncontrollable)
"I lose because I'm not cut out for this."			
"My coach is a bad one. That's why we lose!"			
"I didn't try hard enough."			
"The other players were too big and strong."			
"I didn't kick very well because the crowd was yelling and screaming."			
"I could win if I could buy new cleats."			
"The goal keeper was huge."			
"When I get nervous, I can't play."			
"I was just having a bad day."			

Chapter 13: Development of Motivation and Self-Regulation

ANSWER KEY – ANALYZING ATTRIBUTIONS

Think about Willy from *Willy the Wizard* (Browne, 2003) and analyze each of the following attributions with respect to locus, stability, and controllability. The first one has been completed for you.

After a success Willy says…I was successful because…

	Locus: (internal or external)	Stability: (stable or unstable)	Controllability: (controllable or uncontrollable)
"I'll win every game because I have talent."	I	S	U
"I scored because I was wearing my cleats."	E	U	C
"Soccer is easy!"	E	S	U
"Coach gave me some good plays and I used them to win."	I	U	C
"I won because I had beginner's luck."	E	U	U
"The stranger helped me win."	E	U	U
"My team's really good because we practice."	I	U	C
"My cleats are magic."	E	U	U
"I am a Wizard because I studied the plays coach gave me."	I	U	C
"My team tried super hard and will try hard again next time."	I	U	C

After a failure Willy says…I failed because…

	Locus: (internal or external)	Stability: (stable or unstable)	Controllability: (controllable or uncontrollable)
"I lose because I'm not cut out for this."	I	S	U
"My coach is a bad one. That's why we lose!"	E	S	U
"I didn't try hard enough."	I	U	C
"The other players were too big and strong."	E	U	U
"I didn't kick very well because the crowd was yelling and screaming."	E	U	U
"I could win if I could buy new cleats."	E	U	C
"The goal keeper was huge."	E	U	U
"When I get nervous, I can't play."	I	S	U
"I was just having a bad day."	I	U	U

Chapter 14: Peers, Schools, and Society

Related Picture Book: *Wemberly Worried* by Kevin Henkes

*"Throughout the morning, Wemberly and Jewel sat side by side
and played together whenever they could. '"*

Henkes, 2000

Synopsis: Wemberly worried about big things, little things, and things in-between. She worried about everything; that is, until she met Jewel. Jewel was just like Wemberly. She worried, had a comforting doll, and did many of the same things to self-soothe. Due to common habits and affinities, they identify with each other, ease their transition to school, and become best friends.

Theory or Principle: Peers are individuals of approximately the same age and position within a social group. They make important contributions to youngsters' development—especially in the social-emotional domain. Companionship with peers is a top priority for many children because of the encouragement and understanding provided. Peers buffer children against ridicule and aggressive actions; friendships forged among peers can be lifetime networks of support.

Discussion Questions:
Peers serve many functions in a child's life. Look at the following list of ideas and explain how Jewel provided peer support to Wemberly:

Peers offer emotional support.

Peers serve as partners for practicing social skills.

Peers socialize one another.

Peers contribute to a sense of identity.

Children form friendships with their peers and these friendships have four qualities. Friendships are voluntary, reciprocal, powered by shared routines, and offer mutual support. Explain how the friendship between Wemberly and Jewel revealed these qualities.

As children grow and develop, so do their friendships. Explain the characteristics of friendship that a child Wemberly's age (preschool) might exhibit.

What characteristics of friendship would be expected of children at ages different than Wemberly's (infancy, middle childhood, early adolescence, late adolescence)?

How will you support peer relationships among the children in your care?

Chapter 14: Peers, Schools, and Society
Collaborative Activity: Assessing Learning Communities

Related Picture Book: *T is for Teachers: A School Alphabet* by Steven and Deborah Layne

> *"Inside every schoolhouse there's much to do and see.*
> *Let's look at all that makes school fun; we'll work from A to Z."*
>
> Layne & Layne, 2005

Synopsis: All the things and people who make up what we think of as "school" are explored, letter-by-letter, through poetry and expository text.

Theory or Principle: Children are more apt to thrive in "learning communities" that are warm and supportive, are led by teachers who care and express support for learning, and that actively involve students in collaborative learning. Schools that operate as true communities encourage everyone to work together as productive citizens. A teacher's values and expectations are interpreted by students through a "hidden curriculum" as well as stated expectations for behavior and achievement.

Materials: Multiple copies of *T Is for Teachers: A School Alphabet* or a "page spread" for each group. You might purchase two copies of the book, cut the pages out, and give each group a page spread from the original. It is necessary to have two copies because the pages are double-sided.

Directions: Each group works on one or two letters (a page or a page spread) from the picture book. There are 17 page spreads, so group students accordingly.

Students examine the illustrations and read the text to discover evidence of:
 ➢ a productive (or unproductive) classroom climate
 ➢ developmentally appropriate methods and tasks
 ➢ school traditions
 ➢ school values
 ➢ teachers communicating high expectations

Encourage groups to use their textbook to support their decisions. Each group records its findings on the following assessment page and then shares its responses to the large group, in alphabetical order.

Chapter 14: Peers, Schools, and Society

Collaborative Activity: Assessing Learning Communities

_____ is for _____ and _____ is for _____
From *T is for Teachers: A School Alphabet* (2005) by Steven and Deborah Layne
The School as a Community
Classroom Climate:
Developmentally Appropriate Methods and Tasks:
School Traditions:
Socialization in Schools
School Values:
Communicating High Expectations:

References

Ainsworth, M., with Blehar, M., Waters, E., & Wall, S. (1978). *Patterns of*

    attachment. Hillsdale, NJ: Erlbaum.

Aliki. (1998). *Marianthe's story.* New York: Greenwillow Books.

Arnold, T. (1997). *Parts.* New York: Scholastic.

Bandura, A. (1963). The role of imitation in personality. *The Journal of Nursery*

    Education, 18(3).

Bang, M. (1999). *When Sophie gets angry – really, really, angry.* New York:

    Scholastic.

Bosak, S.V., & McGaw, L. (2003). *Something to remember me by: A story about love*

    and legacies. New York: Scholastic.

Bronfenbrenner, U., & Ceci, S. J. (1994). Nature-nurture reconceptualized in

    developmental perspective: A bioecological model. *Psychological Review*

    (101): 568-586.

Browne, A. (2000). *Willy the dreamer.* Boston: Walker Books.

Browne, A. (2003). *Willy the wizard.* Cambridge, MA: Candlewick Press.

Cusimano, M. (2001). *You are my I love you.* New York: Penguin Press.

Danneberg, J. (2003). *First year letters.* Watertown, MA: Charlesbridge.

Erikson, E. (1959). *Identity and the life cycle.* New York: International

    Universities Press.

Fierstein, H., & Cole, H. (2002). *The sissy duckling.* New York: Simon & Schuster.

Fox, M. (1985). *Wilfred Gordon McDonald Partridge.* Brooklyn, NY: Kane/Miller.

Frasier, D. (1991). *On the day you were born.* Orlando, FL: Harcourt.

Freud, S. (1924). The dissolution of the Oedipus Complex. *Standard Edition (19):*

    172-179.

Freymann, S., & Elffers, J. (1999). *How are you peeling? Foods with moods.* New

    York: Scholastic.

Galdone, P. (1972). *The three bears.* New York: Clarion Books.

Gardner, H. (1999). *Intelligence reframed: Multiple intelligences for the 21st*

    century. New York: Basic Books.

Geisel, T. S. (Dr. Seuss). (1975). *Oh, the thinks you can think!* New York: Random

    House.

Gerstein, M. (2002). *The wild boy.* New York: Farrar, Straus and Giroux.

Gilligan, C. (1982). *In a different voice.* Cambridge, MA: Harvard.

Harris, R. (1996). *Happy birth day.* Cambridge, MA: Candlewick Press.

Henkes, K. (1993). *Owen.* New York: Greenwillow Books.

Henkes, K. (1996). *Lilly's purple plastic purse.* New York: Scholastic.

Henkes, K. (2000). *Wemberly worried*. New York: Scholastic.

Itard, J.-M. G. *The wild boy of Aveyron*. Paris: Goujon Brothers, 1801.

Kohlberg, L., Levine, C., & Hewer, Alexandra. (1983). *Moral stages: A current formulation and a response to critics*. Basel, New York: Karger.

Kraus, R. (1971). *Leo the late bloomer*. New York: Simon and Schuster.

Layne, S. L., & Layne, D. D. (2005). *T is for teachers: A school alphabet*. Chelsea, MI: Sleeping Bear Press.

Lester, H. (1999). *Hooway for Wodney Wat*. Boston: Houghton Mifflin.

LeVine, E. (1989). *I hate English*. New York: Scholastic.

Lionni, L. (1970). *Fish is fish*. New York: Scholastic.

London, J. (2000). *Froggy bakes a cake*. New York: Scholastic.

Lovell, P. (2001). *Stand tall, Molly Lou Melon*. New York: Scholastic.

Martin, B. Jr., & Archambault, J. (1987). *Knots on a counting rope*. New York: Scholastic.

McDonald, M. (1995). *Insects are my life*. New York: Orchard Books.

Munsch, R. (1986). *Love you forever*. Scarborough, ON: Firefly Books.

National Middle School Association, http://www.nmsa.org .

Piaget, J. (1924). *Judgment and reasoning in the child*. London: Routledge & Kegan Paul edition, published in 1928.

Piaget, J. (1936). *Origins of intelligence in the child.* London: Routledge & Kegan

Paul edition, published in 1953.

Piaget, J. (1957). *Construction of reality in the child.* London: Routledge & Kegan

Paul.

Piaget, J., & Inhelder, B. (1955). *Growth of logical thinking.* London: Routledge &

Kegan Paul edition, published in 1958.

Polacco, P. (1994). *Pink and Say.* New York: Scholastic.

Polacco, P. (1998). *Thank you, Mr. Falker.* New York: Scholastic.

Rosales, M. (1996). *'Twas the night b'fore Christmas.* New York: Scholastic.

Scieszka, J., & Smith, L. (1995). *Math curse.* New York: Viking.

Shannon, D. (1999). *No, David!* New York: Scholastic.

Shannon, D. (2002). *David gets in trouble.* New York: Scholastic.

Skinner, B. F. (1938). *The behavior of organisms: An experimental analysis.*

Cambridge, MA: B. F. Skinner Foundation edition, published in 1999.

Smith, H. L. (1998). Literacy and instruction in African American communities:

Shall we overcome? In B. Pérez (ed.), *Sociocultural contexts of language and

literacy.* Mahwah, NJ: Erlbaum.

Snihura, U. (1998). *I miss Franklin P. Shuckles.* Toronto, ON: Annick Press.

Viorst, J. (1972). *Alexander and the terrible, horrible, no good, very bad day.* New

    York: Scholastic.

Vygotsky, L. S. (1934). *Thought and language.* Cambridge, MA: MIT edition

    published in 1962.

Waddell, M. (1989). *Once there were giants.* New York: Delacorte Press.